THE AUXILIARY FIRE SERVICE

Ron Henderson

Nostalgia Road Publications

CONTENTS

The **Nostalgia Road** Series ™

is produced under licence by

Nostalgia Road Publications Ltd.
Unit 6, Chancel Place, Shap Road Industrial Estate,
Kendal, Cumbria, LA9 6NZ
Tel. +44 (0)1539 738832 - Fax: +44 (0)1539 730075

designed and published by
Trans-Pennine Publishing Ltd.
PO Box 10, Appleby-in-Westmorland, Cumbria, CA16 6FA
Tel. +44 (0)17683 51053 Fax. +44 (0)17683 53558
e-mail: admin@transpenninepublishing.co.uk

and printed by
Kent Valley Colour Printers Ltd.
Kendal, Cumbria - +44 (0)1539 741344

© Text: Trans-Pennine Publishing Ltd. 2006
© Photographs: Author's collection or as credited

Front Cover: *This preserved war-time Bedford heavy unit was representative of the vehicles issued to the AFS in the early post-war era until the arrival of the new generation Green Goddesses.* J. Clish

Rear Cover Top: *Pumping from open water through a six-inch hose in the heart of Northumberland's Kielder Forest, a regular training venue for north east AFS personnel. This Green Goddess was part of Sunderland Fire Brigade's fleet.*

Rear Cover Bottom: *Another example of a war-time Bedford heavy unit. This one operated with the North Riding of Yorkshire Fire Brigade post-war and later with the Smiths Dock Company, Middlesbrough before being acquired for preservation.*

Title Page: *Kielder Forest in Northumberland was a regular training area for members of Northumberland County Fire Brigade. Two Northumberland Green Goddesses participate in a water relay exercise in a most picturesque location.*

This Page: *An Austin K2 ATV, towing a Dennis large trailer pump heads a convoy of early post-war AFS appliances on the A38 at Lulsgate during* Exercise Vanguard *in 1953.* N. Tarling collection.

INTRODUCTION

The post-war Auxiliary Fire Service (AFS), part of Britain's civil defence system, was established in 1949 as a civilian means of deterrent following the end of World War II. With the increasing development of the atomic and hydrogen bombs, came the threat that the country would suffer untold damage and casualty loss from the devastation caused by these weapons. To this end a huge recruitment campaign and emergency vehicle building programme was established to provide sufficient manpower and material resources, which in turn could be mobilised to any part of the country and be self-sufficient whilst engaged in fire and rescue duties. However, historically the AFS originated before the war even though it only had a short existence before the war-time fire brigades were nationalised.

Above: *Some General Purpose Lorries were used to carry inflatable portable dams by the AFS. One such dam is seen in the process of being filled from an open water supply, from which the Green Goddess could in turn draw water for relaying to the fire ground.*

This book briefly describes the pre-war origination of the Emergency Fire Brigade organisation, and it was this organisation that first saw a nationwide campaign to recruit auxiliary firemen and women in a massive pre-war expansion programme. The account continues with the postwar re-establishment, development and final disbanding of one of the country's most illustrious organisations.

Ron Henderson   Washington, April 2006

FOUNDATION

In February 1937, the Home Office issued a manual on Emergency Fire Brigade Organisation to one thousand fire authorities asking them to consider the problem of war-time risks and the consideration of drawing up individual precaution schemes. The Air Raid Precautions Act that followed empowered the Home Secretary with central authority, and imposed upon County and County Borough councils the duty of preparing 'Air raid general precaution schemes.' County Borough and Urban District Councils were asked to submit proposals for the extinction of fires likely to be caused by air raids and for the protection of life and property.

The memorandum further advised of a proposed massive expansion, by means of which the Government would provide the necessary pumps and equipment on free loan. The local authorities approached were required to submit proposals on the establishment of auxiliary fire stations, the recruitment and training of auxiliary firemen, and the provision of additional water supplies and communication systems. They were also given a yardstick for the preparation of their schemes, which was based on the mileages within the individual districts and whether these risks were of low, medium or high category. From the results of these surveys, a determination was made on the number of pumps and manpower that would be required to deal with any subsequent air raids.

Top Left: *Until the advent of standard towing vehicles, the government grants that were available permitted local authorities to purchase second-hand cars of 30-cwt, of which many interesting conversions took place. This American Packard is attached to a Sigmund trailer pump operated in the Edinburgh region.* I. Scott collection

Middle Left: *Another Packard car conversion. Rather than tow a trailer pump behind this vehicle, it was enclosed in the rear passenger compartment and boot. The firemen were accommodated in rearward facing seats in front of the pump.* N. Tarling collection

Bottom Left: *The Office of Works new fire service appliance building programme commenced with a series of heavy pumping units, initially mounted onto four wheel trailers. One hundred and twenty were constructed in this way, but most were later remounted onto fireboats.*
J. C. Thompson collection

Top Right: *Dunfermline in Scotland adapted one of the brigade's vans to tow their heavy pump unit mounted onto an Acedes trailer. The configuration of the deliveries on this pump is unusual.* I. Scott collection

Middle Right: *Subsequent heavy pump units were mounted onto self-propelled chassis, and one of the earliest examples of this being the Morris Commercial carrying a self-contained pump.* N. Tarling collection

Bottom Right: *Fordson was also a popular choice for mounting the heavy pumps. The pump on this Stockbridge, Edinburgh example has only the engine enclosed, the pump mechanism being exposed.* I. Scott collection

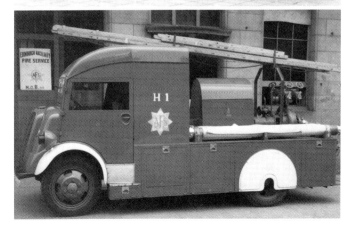

The proposals also envisaged a scheme whereby sufficient trailer pumps and crews would patrol the streets of a town at ten minute intervals and shorter intervals in the high-risk areas during emergencies, so that fires could be quickly identified and extinguished. A proposal that very quickly brought the response that no-one in his right senses would dream of such a proceeding. The Government initially fixed the number of auxiliaries at two hundred thousand. In London alone it was determined that there was a need for thirty thousand auxiliary firemen and two thousand, eight hundred emergency pumps!

This supplement to the established fire brigades was really the forerunner of the Auxiliary Fire Service. Under the proposals pumps and equipment were to be supplied on free loan, but the training of the personnel was to be done locally with the aid of government grants. The first London AFS man was not recruited until March 1938, despite the fact that in the rest of the country 30,000 people had already offered their services. This unpaid cadre of men undertook training on weekends and evenings, and in a very short time the regular fire service personnel were outnumbered by the volunteers. Women were also recruited to take over control and watch room duties, drive staff cars and perform any other duties that would release firemen for active fire-fighting duties. In early-1937, The Commissioners of His Majesty's Works & Public Buildings invited tenders for 'considerable numbers of Motor Driven Fire Pumps' of the following capacities: -

(1)	Heavy,	Approx. 700/900gpm.
(2)	Large,	Approx. 350/500gpm.
(3)	Medium,	Approx. 250/300gpm.
(4)	Light,	Approx. 120/150gpm.
(5)	Light Portable,	Approx. 50/75gpm.

Above: *Fordson 7V and Austin K4 chassis became the choice for the war-time escape carriers. A line up of early Fordsons with John Morris escapes is pictured awaiting distribution at the Cheshire firm of Jennings Ltd.* I.Scott collection

The heavy pumps were to be mounted on frames for conveyance on lorries or four-wheeled trailer chassis, whilst the large, medium and light pumps were to be mounted on two-wheeled chassis for towing; the light ones had to be capable of being carried over rough ground by two men.

The new government-issued pumps to meet these new requirements were a complete departure from the conventional peace-time appliances, being either trailer-mounted for towing behind suitable light vehicles or on motor chassis with separate motors for the road engine and pumping equipment. The pumping unit was also supplied for fixed mounting in an industrial establishment or on a boat. As the construction process continued, massive orders were placed with various British manufacturers.

Initially three makes, Bedford, Fordson and Morris Commercial chassis were utilised for the 750gpm self-propelled pumping units, but these were later joined by others from the Austin Motor Company. They were supplied to local authorities as they became available from the manufacturers, all were painted in Battleship Grey.

The self-propelled pumps were basically a standard lorry chassis/cab with separate engine-driven pump on the rear. Hose and equipment lockers were built into the sides and a separate cab (with open back and rear-facing seats) was provided for the crew. Pumping equipment was provided by Leyland-powered Gwynne units or Tangye and Sulzer pumps that featured engines by Ford. By March of 1938 Leyland Motors had produced and distributed 50 to fire brigades in various parts of the country including ten to London. The introduction of the pumps caused bitter criticisms in fire brigade circles regarding the two separate driving units and it was often asked 'that if the appliances were to be self-propelled, why not adhere to the standard peace-time practice of one engine driving both road wheels?'

Top Right: *Thousands of trailer pumps were constructed during the years leading up to the start of the war. This Standard Gwynne Light Trailer was issued to Galashiels in 1939.* I. Scott collection

Middle Right: *Hose-laying lorries, capable of paying out miles of hose, whilst they were moving, formed an important part of the war-time fire engine program as this Bedford-built example shows; others were built on the Fordson 7V chassis.*

Bottom Right: *In order to replace or supplement the many types of rudimentary towing vehicles, large orders were placed with Austin and Ford for purpose-built 'auxiliary towing vehicles.' The lighter Ford vehicles, illustrated here with a Dennis large trailer pump, were very much in the minority.* N. Tarling collection

The reason for this alteration to practice, was that the programme was so vast and the urgency so great that it was deemed both quicker and cheaper to use this method, even though two engines were required instead of one. A letter reproduced in *Fire* magazine, by a reader with an engineering degree had nothing to say in favour of this Home Office fire engine for air raid purposes. It was described as, "having a cumbersome power-unit and pump weighing just on a ton, with a prime mover that developed 29.4hp and consumed five and one half gallons of petrol an hour." Apparently no-one with any sense "would dream of having one of these things on his mind where peace-time fire defence is involved." As the war progressed the extra heavy pump unit with a capacity of 1,100-gpm was introduced for conveyance by the same means as the smaller unit. These heavier pumps had six deliveries as opposed to four on the standard heavy unit.

As well as the 'Queen Anne's Mansions on Wheels' (as the new self-propelled appliances were nicknamed), huge orders were placed for trailer pumps with firms like Beresford-Stork, Coventry Climax, Dennis, Sigmund and Worthington-Simpson. These trailer-mounted pumps, with various outputs and categorised as either, light, medium or large were seen to be advantageous because of the economy of initial cost and their manoeuvrability over rough terrain that conventional appliances could not traverse. Disadvantages though were that a towing unit was needed to transport the apparatus. So far as these pumps were concerned, the Government was of the opinion that in the event of war enough high-powered private cars would be available by requisition, purchase or gift to tow them.

Above: *A typical example of a war-time requisitioned vehicle is this Bedford lorry converted into a foam tender. The cab doors have been removed to facilitate rapid entry and exit and ensure a speedy response.* J. C. Thompson collection

In practice this was not always the case though. One chief fire officer scoured his town for commercial vehicles in the eight-cwt to 40-cwt range and found that every mechanically propelled vehicle had been earmarked by the Ministry of Transport for other purposes than fire duty. Another approached 60 large businesses for the same purposes and received a similar fruitless response. Apparently the Military had the first choice and for the rest it was a matter of 'first come, first served.'

It was estimated that around 20,000 emergency pumps would be needed to protect the air raid risks in the cities, but there was criticism levied at the initial trailer pump orders. Questions were raised regarding orders placed with Sigmund of Czechoslovakia, who had been contracted to supply 1,000 of the initial 3,410 pumps ordered, as some asked whether British manufacturers had been afforded the opportunity to participate in the scheme.

Sigmund therefore opened a plant in Gateshead, Co. Durham from where the company name would later become more significant in the post-war AFS era. In all 24 firms tendered to supply trailer pumps and four were initially awarded contracts, but others were also given contracts as the war progressed. By October of 1938 almost 6,000 assorted pumps and over 900 miles of hose had been ordered by the Home Office. Trailer pumps were being turned out at the rate of 90 per month.

Another, more conventional type of appliance, the escape carrier, was then ordered by the Home Office. These were based on Austin and Fordson chassis, following the construction of a prototype on a Morris Commercial chassis. This type of appliance, was equipped with a small water tank and hose reel equipment and each carried a 50' wheeled escape together with facilities to tow a trailer pump. Initially, 70 were ordered in August 1939 with 25 of these being assigned to London. Future orders were later modified to exclude the fitting of a water tank and hose reel equipment. As the war progressed and in light of experiences, these appliances were later refitted with the first aid equipment and American-made Barton pumps.

These were imported for mounting onto the front of the engine, and as a consequence did away with the need to tow a trailer pump. Many other appliances were issued and there was much improvisation by AFS personnel with their motly stock of vehicles. but before the country's fire brigades were nationalised one other notable class of appliances to be delivered were the turntable ladders. Before the war the Germans had become adept at manufacturing and exporting elevating ladders to Britain in competition with Merryweather & Sons. On account of the latter's appliances being more expensive than their German counterparts, orders were placed with both Metz in Germany and Merryweather for 20 turntable ladders each. As the international situation deteriorated it was no longer possible to obtain German supplies, so Merryweather became the sole supplier of this type of appliance during the war years under the Emergency Fire Brigade Scheme. Orders were thus placed for a variety of machines with 100' ladders on Leyland TLM and Dennis chassis. Some later batches were based on the Leyland's TD7 bus chassis fitted with petrol engines and also (unusually) diesel-powered vehicles based on Leyland's TSC18 coach chassis with an enclosed cab Also, a new basic design, was a batch of 50, hand-operated 60' ladders mounted onto Austin K4 chassis. There were a total of 100 ladders in the UK before the war, 13 of them in London, but the brigade there said these numbers needed to be supplemented by a further 42 appliances Most of these war-time turntable ladders saw out the war, with many of them remaining in service until the mid 1960s.

To maintain adequate water supplies during air-raids, many local authorities set up Emergency Water Supplies (EWS). To supplement these a new type of emergency fire appliance was introduced, the mobile dam unit (MDU) that consisted of a flat bed lorry on which was carried a 500-gallon water tank. These MDUs needed to tow a trailer pump, so the question of suitable towing vehicles became an urgent necessity as war became more certain. In London proposals were made to hire 2,000 taxicabs for the purpose. Many other vehicles were requisitioned and used as improvised fire engines, and some interesting conversions of lorries and vans appeared to supplement the emergency pumps being issued by the Government.

Accommodation also became a pressing problem as the strength of some brigades was increased more than ten-fold and garages, schools, disused factories and even railway arches were requisitioned or hired for the accommodation of appliances and personnel. Even these adaptations were not without problems, for instance there were problems with property-owners not being paid rent dues as swiftly as was anticipated.

As the threat of war increased, many of the former volunteers became paid members of the fire service. By September 1939 89,000 men and 6,000 women had been mobilised for full-time service, whilst 14,000 emergency pumps were then available. Initially the early war years were a relatively quiet period, although a major air raid caused a fire at Pembroke Docks in August 1940, igniting several oil storage tanks which burned for 17 days and resulted in the death of five auxiliary firemen, the first fire service casualties of the war. By that time the huge orders for emergency pumps was almost complete, with 24,000 appliances (including 4,000 for the Admiralty, War Office, Air Ministry and other departments) having been delivered.

Concentrated air raids, on London especially, then became more frequent and on 7th September 1940 West Ham became the first brigade to put the Regional Reinforcement Scheme into action requesting 500 pumps to fight fires raging along the banks of the River Thames. This then became the norm with frequent raids taxing the brigades to the limit with reinforcing moves bringing in appliances from as far away as Birmingham. Between 7th September and 2nd November 1940, London was bombed for 57 consecutive nights by an average of 200 bombers every night. As the year progressed other cities became victim to the raiders, including Birmingham, Bristol, Clydebank, Coventry, Liverpool and Manchester. During the latter raid, so many of the Manchester's towing vehicles were out of service, that the firemen had to resort to pulling the pumps by hand.

This episode (in December 1940) resulted in the introduction of one of the most famous and long lasting standard war-time fire appliances, the Auxiliary Towing Vehicle. An initial order was placed for 2,000 vehicles based on an Austin two-ton K2 chassis, plus 200 lighter types based on Ford's military chassis (the Fordson W0T2). The vehicles were fitted with a box body, inside which the firemen were accommodated together with their hose and items of equipment. An extension ladder was carried on the roof and a trailer pump was towed behind. Nearly 6,000 of these ATVs were made and some were still in service with peace-time fire brigades until the late 1960s.

As the war progressed, the air raids became more frequent, especially on cities outside London, and as a result reinforcing moves became more frequent with fire appliances travelling many miles to support beleaguered colleagues with smaller establishments. However, with these mutual aid schemes came many other problems such as different conditions of service, rank markings, incompatible equipment, the issues of hierarchies and local influence that prevailed amongst the many hundreds of separate fire authorities.

NATIONALISATION AND RE-BIRTH

By 1941 the AFS had more than 20,000 mobile pumps and more than 3,000 miles of canvas delivery hose. In addition there were nearly 700 miles of extension ladders in sizes of 40, 30 and 16 feet, but it was all to very soon change. To more effectively manage this huge influx of men and machines and to consolidate all the variations inherent in the individual brigades the biggest change ever to take place in the history of the British fire services occurred on the 18th August 1941 when the 1,440 individual fire authorities in Great Britain were nationalised and divided into 55 force areas, six of them in Scotland.

The Auxiliary Fire Service therefore ceased to exist as a separate entity and was wholly incorporated into the National Fire Service (NFS) coming under one Department, controlled by the Home Office.

At the end of the war the NFS was disbanded following the suspension of the Civil Defence (Suspension of Powers) Act 1945. Even though changes in fire cover began in 1945, it was not until 1948 that the service was handed back to the local authorities, and then not in the same format as before the war. Indeed, new county fire authorities were established reducing the number of pre-war fire brigades to 135. However, the stand down of the Civil Defence was short-lived, as increased threats from Russia and associated Iron Curtain countries and the onset of the Cold War resulted in the Civil Defence Act (1948) being passed, thus reconstituting the Civil Defence Corps and the Auxiliary Fire Service. The objective of this was to enable a civil defence organisation for the purpose of affording protection against hostile attack. It also included any measures (not amounting to actual combat), for affording defence against any form of hostile attack by a foreign power.

Left: *During the early post-war period, standard war-time appliances were used to equip the resurrected AFS. Austin ATVs and trailer pumps were re-issued to the local authority fire brigades, and one is seen receiving attention to its bell.*

Top Right: *Here is an early post-war AFS convoy, as a van-bodied Austin ATV tows a trailer pump during an exercise in County Durham.* CD&DFRA

Middle Right: *Another view of the same convoy as it passes the photographer, this time showing another style of body on the Austin chassis, which is followed by Bedford and Fordson 7V heavy units. The crews have declined the comforts of the rearward-facing shelter behind the cab.* CD&DFRA

Bottom Right *An impressive post-war turn out of a late-model Fordson heavy unit from Middlesex Fire Brigade. The vehicle is unchanged from its original condition and whilst the driver and officer in charge have the benefit of an enclosed cabin, the remainder of the crew were accommodated in an open shelter, directly behind the cab.* N. Tarling collection

In November 1949, voluntary recruitment (on similar lines to that occurring pre-war) commenced, as fire authorities were told to recruit two male auxiliaries for every whole-time member of their brigade and one for every part-time member. Women were also included and it was suggested that they should form 10% of the then current fire brigade establishments. Nationally, the predicted demand was for a total of 50,000 men and 5,000 women. Initially recruitment proved very slow despite heavy advertising campaigns featuring the distribution of pamphlets and posters. These auxiliaries were to be members of the individual local authority fire brigades, but it was stressed that there was no intention of employing them in place of regular firemen to provide fire cover in peace-time. Proposals were also made for the provision of 5,000 self-propelled fire appliances, including hose and ancillary equipment for use by the new volunteer fire -fighting force at a cost of twenty million pounds.

It was suggested that a future war would feature the atomic bombing of Britain's cities and their inhabitants. If evidence of the kind of devastation were needed, most people could recall the bombs dropped on Hiroshima and Nagasaki in Japan towards the end of World War II. The energy released at Nagasaki was equivalent to an explosion of 20,000-tons of TNT, with the heat flash being capable of igniting fabrics some two miles distant and complete devastation in a one mile radius.

Top Left: *Trailer pumps of various makes were allocated to the post-war AFS brigades and in Northumberland this Sigmund Morris unit is seen being put to work at one of the brigade's annual drill competitions.* NFRS

Middle Left: *Recruitment of personnel in sufficient numbers was an ongoing problem throughout the existence of the post-war AFS and many recruiting campaigns were organised. Durham County Fire Brigade used this ATV and fitted it with roof-mounted loudspeakers in an effort to attract the attention of potential recruits.* CD&DFRA

Bottom Left: *Here is one of the war-time issue Fordson 7Vs used for feeding fire service personnel. This was an important consideration during exercises and prolonged fire-fighting operations. The war-time mobile kitchens, originally purchased with funds from Canadian and South American donors, continued to be used until the advent of new units.*

To deal with such devastation, fire fighting arrangements were supposed to be different to those that prevailed between 1939-1945. For a start, the firemen and appliances would have to be positioned outside the target area and move in to it as a comprehensive force after the attack. It was this theory that formulated the establishment of mobile fire columns, which would each consist of over 600 men and 90 vehicles to include radio facilities, petrol tankers, mobile kitchens and hose-layers. In other words, a self-sufficient force, that could be dispersed around affected areas and operate from their base for long periods of time.

The new Civil Defence Corps became the main theme at the 1950 Lord Mayor's Show in London on 9th November, so 1,200 feet of space in the procession was allocated to the London Fire Brigade. They provided 150 male and female auxiliaries together with a contingent of regular firemen, plus five heavy units (including one representing an AFS recruiting centre), a mobilising centre tableau and a tableau representing fire scenes after an air raid. The remainder of the allocated space was made up with the latest London Fire Brigade appliances and a further selection of heavy units at the rear.

By August 1951 there was a marked paucity of recruits, not only to the AFS but also to the Civil Defence as a whole. In Sheffield the number of auxiliaries required was 356, yet despite 5,000 personal letters, numerous public meetings, film and poster publicity and practical demonstrations, a total of just 136 men and 55 women had been recruited.

TRAINING & DEVELOPMENT

Other Chief Fire Officers expressed similar concerns and they reported that former AFS members were unwilling to volunteer again owing to past experiences. In Oxford, an intense campaign over twelve months saw just 14 men and one woman enroll against a required establishment of 145 men and five women. Durham County Fire Brigade did well with its intensive recruiting drive, but they had employed several mobile recruiting units throughout the county supported by officers giving talks in factory canteens and public gatherings, along with posters and special slide presentations in cinemas. These actions increased recruitment by 200% and by mid-1951 it had nearly reached its quota.

In neighbouring Northumberland it was decided that the drastic situation of recruitment for the AFS demanded the full exploitation of the mobility and ingenuity of the fire brigade, so starting in Morpeth, every town and many villages were given demonstrations of fire brigade equipment dating from the 18th-century to the present day.

Above: *Without doubt the Bedford Green Goddess was the best known vehicle in the new post-war building program. The prototype was introduced in 1952 and differed from the production models by having hinged doors all round and an illuminated fire sign, as opposed to the twin orange blinker warning lights.* N. Tarling collection

In addition, a mobile exhibition van was used to carry topical and museum exhibits. These publicity events resulted in the recruitment of 100 volunteers from the 5,000 people that visited the exhibition. Even so, according to the Home Secretary, by the end of the year, only one third of the minimum number of civil defence workers that would be needed in peace-time to ensure rapid expansion of the service in an emergency, had so far been enrolled.

To stimulate interest, a recruiting film entitled *The Waking Point* was produced and it previewed in London in November 1951. The film, concerned mainly with rescue services, was available for both general release in cinemas and for local authority recruiting campaigns.

Top Left: *The bare chassis and scuttle of a Bedford S-Type model as it was delivered to the coachbuilders to re-appear later as one of the new generation emergency pumps. The power take off transmission to operate the pump can be clearly seen.* J. C. Thompson collection

Bottom Left: *This is part of an early batch of AFS appliances, which was bodied by Weymann (note; early examples were registered in the LYO series). It was taken to the Plaxton coach-builder's factory in Scarborough so that this company could see a finished product.* J. C. Thompson collection

Large-scale exercises were a frequent event in the calendar of the embryo post-war Auxiliary Fire Service involving large convoy runs, followed by a simulated attack on some British town or city. In July 1951, *Exercise Tripod*, the biggest AFS manoeuvre since the war saw two companies of London auxiliary firemen, plus a detachment of fire women, leave London's Lambeth headquarters on a reinforcing exercise to Portsmouth. Twenty pumps, together with ancillary vehicles made the long journey taking a night stop at Goodwood before continuing to Portsmouth Dockyard whereupon they reinforced units of the city AFS putting 40 jets into play to protect assigned establishments. Simulating an actual reinforcing move to an area under attack, the exercise also provided practical experience in the movement of appliances in convoy, along with procedures at a reinforcing base, feeding arrangements, fuel and maintenance of appliances and the general administrative organisation. A similar event occurred during the following year when 60 pumps and ancillary vehicles from the London regions of Essex, Kent, Middlesex, Surrey, Croydon and West Ham travelled from London to Folkestone, where *Exercise Flair* supposed that the town had been heavily bombarded from the air. An additional ten pumps arrived from Kent to formulate five companies, each one given a sector of the town where a large fire and several smaller ones were tackled. The exercise culminated in 60 jets being put to work in the harbour area.

In October 1951, 175 auxiliary firemen from Kent (equipped with 21 pumps from 19 stations) took part in *Medfire*, a large-scale exercise that supposed an attack on an urban settlement, Medtown, where it was assumed that a disused lime works by the River Medway had been plastered with high explosive and incendiary bombs. Twenty-four fires were specially prepared using waste oil, tar and old tyres and after each fire had been extinguished, a larger fire was started in which all crews had a job to do, either by relaying water or actually tackling the fire.

Similar events were occurring in all parts of the country. In July 1952, 55 appliances were drawn from the fire brigades of Huddersfield Corporation and the West Riding of Yorkshire County Council stations of Harrogate, Pontefract, Keighley, Mexborough and Cleckheaton formed two mobile columns to deal with 'assumed' fires in Huddersfield with a similar event taking place at Sheffield in September.

On Merseyside, Liverpool's auxiliaries took part in a mock blitz in the city's docklands, where they were supported by fire fighters from Southport, Stockport, Bolton, Oldham Manchester and Salford. This was the biggest exercise of its type on Merseyside since World War II and comprised of an attendance of over 50 appliances. The northeast of England's biggest exercise to date occurred in Newcastle upon Tyne.

Above: *Several different coachbuilders were contracted to build the thousands of new generation civil defence fire engines that euphemistically became known as the Green Goddesses. This example was bodied by Jennings of Sandbach and it demonstrates the facilities for loading and unloading the portable pump.* N.Tarling collection

Exercise Tyne on the quaysides of Newcastle and Gateshead saw five simulated fires in riverside properties whereupon a total of 55 pumps, five hundred fire service members and two hundred civil defence workers plus turntable ladder and fireboat attended from 13 different brigades, including Cumberland & Westmorland during which 150 jets of water were called into play.

Top Left: *The Green Goddesses were all adorned with standard AFS insignia, plus the name (in red script) of the brigade to which it was allocated. This one was assigned to the Soke of Peterborough County Council Fire Brigade.* N.Tarling collection

Middle Left: *An innovation with the new AFS appliances was the development by Coventry Climax of an exhaust ejector lightweight pump, which fire-fighters were able to carry to areas inaccessible to conventional fire appliances as admirably illustrated in this photograph.*

Bottom Left: *Here is one of the first new AFS hose-layers built on the Bedford S-Type chassis. Known colloquially as the Big Bedford, this model had only been released at the 1950 Commercial Motor Show and was therefore a thoroughly modern unit at the time. The double deck compartments (where the flaked hose was situated) could accommodate half a mile of six-inch diameter hose, capable of being paid out at speeds of up to 30mph.* J. C. Thompson collection

Durham's contribution in March 1953, devised to test mobilising arrangements and boost recruitment was based on a hypothetical incendiary attack on the city's ancient castle, to which two hundred AFS personnel and 25 appliances were mobilised. Scotland was not omitted and also in March, *Exercise Thistle*, again one of the biggest civil defence exercises ever held, saw large forces congregate on a supposed atom bomb attack on Princess Dock, Govan. In May, 300 midland firemen with 60 appliances took part in what was also claimed to be the biggest civil defence exercise of its kind for the fire services, when convoys of appliances assembled at Birmingham and Coventry to mobilise to 'an atom bomb explosion' in the Hockley area of Birmingham.

There were variations to the themes, but all the exercises involved the deployment of large numbers of vehicles and men. Lancashire's contribution was *Exercise Corona* held in South Lancashire in July 1953, which presumed that a state of war had existed for three months. The Fire Service had supposedly been nationalised, and its establishment increased to deal with enemy air attack. If this was not enough it was also assumed that an atom bomb had been dropped on Merseyside. According to the Under Secretary of State for the Home Office, Sir Hugh Lucas-Tooth, *Exercise Gateway* was the biggest to date. It was divided into three phases and used five companies of ten pumps each in Hampshire over three days in October 1953.

Above: *Also revealed at the debut of the new post-war 'atomic' fire engines was the mobile kitchen unit where the entire offside bodywork was hinged to facilitate easy access and provide protection from the elements whilst the fire personnel were being served. The trailer contained coal for the units cooking appliances.* J. C. Thompson

Right: *The Austin A40 was commonly used by post-war fire brigades as a Utility Van or Utility Tender. The AFS was no exception and the first orders for the resurrected post-war AFS included a batch of Austin A40s, and a typical example from Northumberland is pictured here at an exercise in 1955. The Austin A40 came in two guises; the A40 Dorset models, which were in production from 1947 to 1952 and the A40 Somerset that was built between 1952 and 1954. They came as saloon cars, vans, pick-ups, Countryman estates and vans with side windows and additional seats, as seen with this example.*

This exercise mobilised two hundred appliances and over one thousand regular, retained and auxiliary firemen or fire women from Brigades in the south of England. Watched by high officials of the Home Office, the armed forces, constabularies and local authorities, the exercise (which consisted of the assembly of three mobile columns, two from the London region and one from Hampshire) culminated at Southampton Docks where twelve initial incidents in two dock areas were assumed to have occurred. This particular exercise was designed to provide practical experience in moving appliances in convoy and test new multi-channel radio sets, which had been specially designed for mobile columns.

Above: *Field telephone line-laying units and Land Rover towing vehicles were included in the mobile column's inventory. The Brockhouse trailer shown in this picture with its canvas cover removed, clearly shows some of the equipment that the Home Office felt was necessary for the important facility of emergency communications in the event of a nuclear war.* J. C. Thompson collection

In the *Gateway* exercise, the London and Hampshire units were supplemented by those from Berkshire and Reading, Bournemouth, Buckinghamshire, Dorset, Isle of Wight, Oxford City and County, Portsmouth and Southampton.

Top Right: *Recruitment to all branches of the civil defence was not easy, so an ongoing programme and frequent public demonstrations had to be held throughout the country to try and stimulate enrolment numbers. This particular picture shows how Devon County Fire Brigade displayed some of its 'war emergency equipment', and at the same time heavily advertised that many more men and women were needed!* N. Tarling collection

Middle Right: *At the other end of the country, the AFS in Northumberland was a good example of how the recruitment work was done.* NFRS

Bottom Right: *Northumberland County Fire Brigade also had the distinction at one time of recruiting more AFS personnel than any other authority. This was mainly thanks to vigorous advertising campaigns and travelling recruitment centres, which were often held outside large industrial undertakings.* NFRS

An interesting conclusion to this particular exercise was that the return convoy of the London and Home Counties appliances stopped off at Reading for tea, at which they were welcomed by the Lord Mayor and other officials plus a crowd of ten thousand people! In Derbyshire a large-scale exercise was held at Chesterfield in early-1954. *Exercise Spire* (named after Chesterfield's famous church steeple) involved 72 appliances from 13 North or East Midlands brigades. During the same year, equipped with the new vehicles, Bradford Fire Brigade organised an exercise to tackle a simulated atom bomb attack. At this one 250 members of the AFS from throughout Yorkshire were mobilised and a two mile relay of the new six-inch diameter plastic piping was laid in 90-minutes to pump water from Chellow Dene reservoir.

At the end of 1953, the AFS had a total manpower of 19,974, an increase of 4,617 on the previous years figure with the total enrolled in all branches of the Civil Defence exceeding 40,000. The only brigade with more than one thousand volunteers was Lancashire, and it was evident that the AFS lagged woefully in all areas except Northumberland where over three hundred AFS men had been recruited within the previous twelve months by means of a house-to-house recruiting campaign, giving the county the second biggest establishment. London's total was 533. "Civil Defence was part of the nation's defences" declared the Home Secretary to a conference of civic heads and representatives of local authorities in London.

Above: *As well as the Green Goddesses there were hundreds of general-purpose lorries ordered for the post-war AFS and capable of many functions. This example, pictured at Reigate in 1953 was adapted for the carrying of foam.*
J. C. Thompson collection

The Home Secretary said that the Government, believed that the danger of World War II had receded, but the development of civil defence plans came second only in value to preserving peace. However, the future position became more ominous following the development of the hydrogen bomb and an increased radius of damage to 20 miles, with the additional threat of 'fall-out' from nuclear particles. It was evident that this threat could not be met by the recruitment of volunteers in peace-time when each mobile fire column required six hundred men, and one hydrogen bomb dropped on a large city might produce a situation that might require the deployment of over 50 columns. The problem was initially resolved by the Air Ministry agreeing that a number of their reservists would not be required in the initial stages of a war and could therefore be trained as firemen during their reservist obligations.

Following a report from the US Atomic Energy Commission on the effects of H-bomb explosions, together with the White Paper on Defence and various Parliamentary debates, the Government intimated that in a future global war the Fire Service would rapidly expand as a nationalised force with class 'H' Royal Air Force reservists forming an AFS to supplement the regular fire-fighters with the staffing of mobile columns.

It was envisaged that ten thousand would be trained annually, while regular fire fighters received mobile column training at the school attached to Surrey Fire Brigades new headquarters at Reigate. The White Paper also announced the formation of military Mobile Defence Corps, consisting of 48 reserve battalions. Of these, 36 were to be used for ambulance and rescue duties and twelve for fire-fighting, to be under the control of the Home Office via Chief Regional Fire Officers.

In January 1953 the Civil Defence mobile column depot at Epsom, Surrey opened, and this was to form the base of an experimental mobile column composed of one hundred soldiers and 50 airmen who, after training, would be engaged in exercises to be staged in various parts of the country. The reason for using armed forces personnel was that the experiments had to be conducted by whole-time personnel, of which the Civil Defence Corps had none.

The first public parade of a fire service mobile column occurred in London on 3rd December 1953, when the Home Secretary reviewed contingent's of the AFS, Civil Defence Corps, Home Guard and the National Hospital Service Reserve at Horse Guards Parade. This was the largest gathering of Civil Defence Services to be held in London since the end of war back in 1945. The AFS were represented by a detachment of 60 firewomen on foot and a mobile column comprised of the latest new vehicles from London, Croydon, Essex, Hertfordshire, Kent, Middlesex, Surrey and West Ham.

Below: *As well as the larger exercises (such as those described in the text), drill competitions were also a regular feature of the AFS. Here, six 4x2 Green Goddesses are lined up awaiting the call for action with historic Alnwick Castle providing an impressive background.* NFRS

Top Left: *From 1954, the Bedford R-Type four-wheel drive chassis became the norm for future Green Goddess appliances, and illustrated here is the chassis and front scuttle of such a unit prior to its being delivered to the body builder. These chassis featured single rear wheels as opposed to the twin rear wheel sets of the 4x2 vehicles.* J. C. Thompson collection

Middle and Bottom Left: *These two side profile views illustrate the difference between the original 4x2 and later 4x4 versions of the Green Goddess. Of the many differences which can be seen, is that the open hose reel locker has been relocated to the centre of the appliance rather than at the rear, whilst the ground clearance was much greater on the 4x4 version.* J. C. Thompson collection

Once organised, the column toured the country starting in the Medway towns and went via the south coast and the Midlands to Glasgow, Edinburgh, Newcastle-upon-Tyne and back to London via many other cities in between. Whilst out on tour, a large number of experiments were undertaken to test the basis of the best establishment and organisation of mobile columns and to see how they could most effectively deploy them in time of war. This experimental column was disbanded at the end of 1954, after which preparations were begun to start the training of reservists for service with mobile columns.

The intention was to call them RAF reservists and train them in the rudiments of rescue and fire-fighting duties at civil defence or fire service establishments. In the first year 15,000 were to be trained and in the following six years it was hoped to have completed training for 100,000 reservists. The Epsom establishment was extended and additional ones opened up near Leeds for civil defence rescue, and another at Washington Hall in Lancashire for fire fighting.

The latter establishment, a teachers training college, was a former army camp built during the war for American servicemen and covered three acres. After conversion the site contained nine, 40' drill towers, nine drill grounds and nine static water tanks, each holding five hundred gallons of water. For training, the reservists had 30 emergency fire appliances and the site could accommodate five hundred men. The first intake of 250 'H Class' reservists commenced their two-week training course in July 1955 and future plans were made to accommodate five hundred on each course. During their training, the reservists familiarised themselves with basic drills relating to emergency pumps and extension ladders, water relays and first-aid.

Top Right: *Despite the original pre-war controversy over the manufacture of Sigmund pumps, the former Czechoslovakian company was awarded the contract to supply the pumps for the AFS Green Goddesses. In testimony to the efficiency of these units, they were still as efficient and serviceable some 40-years after first being issued.*
J. C. Thompson collection

Middle Right: *The construction of several 4x4 Green Goddesses is seen here whilst underway at the Cambridge plant of Papworth Industries Ltd. The huge post-war AFS building program was probably the largest standard fire appliance contract ever to be awarded.*
J. C. Thompson collection

Bottom Right: *The classic and characteristic powerful lines of one of the 4x4 Green Goddesses, newly out of the paint shop.* J. C. Thompson collection

The course also included demonstrations of turntable ladders and other 'peace-time' appliances and films of notable fire operations, with a view to stimulating their interest in the Fire Service and help attract recruits of the right type for the regular and auxiliary branches of service. An even bigger camp was established in the Cotswolds at Moreton-in-Marsh, Gloucestershire, on the site of a former World War II RAF bomber aerodrome. This Home Office Fire Service Training Centre was regarded as the answer to providing the great bulk of manpower for mobile fire columns in times of emergency.

Initially plans were for selected RAF 'H Class' reservists to spend a fortnight at Washington Hall and then a similar period at Moreton. The establishment housed the trainees in former RAF billets and stored in large aircraft hangars were all the appliances that formed a mobile column. From 1959 onwards, the site became used for training of both local authority and AFS personnel and right up until 1968, fire fighters were instructed in the rudiments of atomic warfare, mobile column work and water relay operations. In later years, after undergoing substantial rebuilding and modernisation, the site became the Fire Service College and is still used today to train regular fire fighters and officers from all over the world. Elsewhere mobile column exercises were tested on a regular basis and in November 1954 the London AFS took part in a convoy run of 50-miles distance from White City Stadium, around Buckinghamshire and Hertfordshire before assembling back in London at the London Fire Brigade's Lambeth headquarters.

Top Left: *Mobile control units were identified by a red and white chequered band and on the early models an illuminating chequered dome on the roof. This later 4x4 example has a hinged mast with red light, shown in the folded position just above the cab.* J. C. Thompson collection

Middle Left: *This line up of Green Goddesses, pictured at the assembly point was part of a mobile column exercise where the greater part of the convoy equipment was formed prior to setting off on its destination.*

Bottom Left: *Similar to the control units was the emergency-communications/stores van used for emergency repairs of field communications equipment. They had reduced glazing in the body and were devoid of the chequered markings.*
 J.C. Thompson collection

By this time it was suggested that the optimum number of vehicles making up a convoy should be set at about 80. Apparently the convoy commander set a 'spanking pace', 42 vehicles passing a checkpoint within two minutes. On this occasion, the despatch riders were women members of the AFS, one of whose motorcycle came to grief, fortunately the rider only suffered minor injuries to her lip. The disabled motorcycle was retrieved by the convoys' maintenance van.

A similar exercise was held in May of the following year, this time to Cambridge and involved appliances from London, Middlesex, Surrey, Essex, Kent, Hertfordshire, Croydon, East Ham and West Ham. Sixty-eight pumps and additional control vehicles arranged in two columns were mobilised on this occasion. A spectacular site no doubt, despite most of the vehicles being of the same type. The Isle of Wight was no exception and (also in May 1955) the largest exercise ever held on the island occurred involving the mobilisation of 200 volunteers to an 'incident' at Sandown, where a three-quarters of a mile water relay was set up from the River Yar (near Brading) to supply 2,000-gallons of water per minute to Sandown Shopping Centre. Predominantly a communications exercise, it provided excellent training to the auxiliary fire women that manned the controls and wireless cars.

On 13th March 1954 much publicity was afforded, following a televised exercise held at Sunderland Wharf, Bermondsey on the River Thames. The civil defence show 'Operation Waterside' illustrated the drill for dealing with an isolated incident, one of many thousands predicted to have been caused by an 'atom bomb explosion' in London's Docklands.

Above: *As well as pumping appliances, turntable ladders were also ordered by the Office of Works for distribution to high-risk areas during World War II. The shortage of raw materials forced some diversions of bus chassis for conversion to fire appliances as this petrol-engined Leyland TD7 appliance with a Merryweather 100' ladder demonstrates. The Battleship Grey livery seen on this preserved example is typical of the war-time models, as are the hooded lights and white paint marks along the leading edges of the vehicle; all being signs of the blackout requirements under what were known as Air Raid Precautions measures.*

Right: *Apart from minor differences, Army emergency pumps were identical to those issued to the AFS. This one illustrated here has metal cages protecting the flashing blue beacons.* S.Palmer

Above:. *The AFS had a wide selection of vehicles, and not just fire appliances, as light commercials, motor-cycles and off-road vehicles also formed a significant part of the establishment. Take, for example, the long wheelbase Austin Gipsy shown at one of the Home Office storage sites. These vehicles were used as radio repeater units and personnel carriers. Some were still being disposed of as late as 2006.* J. C. Thompson

Left: *Heavier commercial vehicles were also employed, such as the rather ungainly Commer Superpoise chassis, which was adopted for use as a general-purpose lorry and had various functions by the AFS. This preserved example was a hose-layer and is seen carrying an incorrect registration number, the 'F' and 'X' being reversed.*

Above: *The arrival of the 'Big Bedford' five-ton truck at the end of 1950 was a major boost in what was otherwise a very difficult period for British commercial vehicle manufactures. So successful was the S-Type, that a four-wheel drive version, the R-Type, was quickly produced for military applications and it was this variant that offered so much potential for vehicles that would need to traverse rough terrain. Here is an early 4x2 mobile control unit, which operated in the Bristol region during its AFS existence and is now preserved.*

Right: *After the disbanding of the AFS, many thousands of appliances were disposed of and some interesting conversions ensued. This 4x4 Goddess fitted with a hydraulic maintenance platform was pictured in a commercial vehicle dealers' yard in Bedfordshire in 1988.*

Above: *It must not be forgotten that the AFS comprised of large numbers of fire-women who followed the fine traditions of those women who had volunteered for duty with the National Fire Service during World War II. Here a bevy of 'fire belles' pose for the camera in company with a control unit and a 1964 Land Rover Safari.* NFRS

Left: *When the first national fire fighters' strike took place in 1977 during the 'winter of discontent', the country saw the widespread issue of Green Goddesses that had been held in 'reserve' since the disbandment of the AFS in 1968. These appliances were used by the armed forces, and after operational difficulties the Goddesses were later fitted with two-tone horns and blue beacons in place of the original twin orange blinker lights and hand-operated bell.* T. Welham

During the exercise on the Thames it was assumed that a tall warehouse at the side of the wharf was on fire, made realistic by the ignition of napalm in dustbins placed beside the window openings. With the aid of a turntable ladder from the regular service, many rescues were undertaken and jets put to work before Civil Defence rescue teams 'extracted' further casualties from beneath a huge heap of debris. At the conclusion of events the Deputy Under Secretary of State remarked that, "we may not have all the men and women we need in the AFS but we've got the quality." In February the experimental mobile column undertook an 800-mile tour from Reigate to Exmouth and back, by way of Bristol and Gloucester to mark the conclusion of an eight-month special course that had taken place at the Surrey Fire Brigade Headquarters at Reigate.

Above: *Frequent mobile column and training exercises formed a regular routine during the existence of the AFS. A convoy of 4x2 Green Goddesses is pictured on the A38 passing Lulsgate near Bristol.* N.Tarling collection

On this occasion, the exercises were made as realistic as possible by getting chief fire officers of the towns and counties en-route to set tactical problems without the prior knowledge of the officers in charge of the column. This required the column commanders to carry out reconnaissance of the scene, then make the necessary decisions and carry out the exercise on unfamiliar territory. This column consisted of 80 officers and firemen, one woman officer and three fire-women being moved in a convoy of 40 vehicles.

Above: *Here is a good illustration of the exercises that were held by the AFS, as the picture shows no less than 15 4x2 Green Goddess, along with one Bedford S-Type (with a control unit body) and an Austin A40 car neatly lined up and ready for action. These appliances are actually part of the Cornwall AFS and are being 'held' at a staging point in the South West prior to the commencement of an AFS exercise.* N. Tarling collection

In the Reigate-Exmouth exercise, water relays of three miles distance and commando tactics, in which hose had to be manhandled up cliffs and over rough ground were some of the tasks undertaken on the tour and the Bikini Unit was used to good effect to pump water from the sea as well as rivers.

In the north east of the country the experiences of convoy work was not as positive. In 1959 a mobile column comprising 57 vehicles drawn from the AFS and Civil Defence left the county of Northumberland for a 121-mile journey to Middleton, Midlothian in Scotland. Experiences on this occasion lead to comments that the column was too unwieldy for, whilst its vehicles had covered over a mile of road in close order at the assembly point, once under way it was spread out over two miles and on occasions three miles.

It was also noted that some vehicles, especially hose-layers and pipe-carriers, appeared under-powered and even slight inclines required the selection of low gears resulting in speeds of little more than walking pace.

AFS Vehicles

The first appliances operated by the post-war AFS were of the war-time standard pattern, with trailer pumps forming the main body of equipment, but there were still problems with the issue of suitable towing vehicles. In many cases trailer pumps only were provided at stations where training was undertaken, until the ubiquitous Austin K2 auxiliary towing vehicles were issued later. The K2s were used for various purposes including personnel transport, fire-fighting and some even became mobile recruiting stations, complete with large roof-mounted loudspeakers to spread the message. The early mobile canteen vans were also based on this chassis. Fordson 7Vs were also issued as hose-layers and canteen vans. The Self-Propelled pumps issued were the controversial war-time heavy units based on Fordson, Austin and Bedford chassis.

Above: *The pipe-carrier was an important accessory regarding the relaying of large quantities of water. The spare wheel on the top was not part of the inventory.* D. Barker

These heavy units were repainted to match the livery of the brigades to which they were assigned but without the individual brigades coat of arms. Whilst many were painted bronze green after the issue of the new generation of civil defence appliances, others remained in the red livery until the disbandment of the service. Despite a new generation of purpose-built appliances the ATV was still a useful asset and these appliances were still in use with the AFS until the organisation disbanded for the second time in 1968.

However, late in 1951 the Home Office placed an order for the production of a substantial number of pumping appliances for use in an emergency, the famous Green Goddesses.

Top Left: *The AFS were adept at moving large volumes of water with the high capacity pumps and large bore hoses. Steel pipes were used to form bridges over which water could be transported without causing disruption to any vehicles that used the roads they spanned.*

Middle Left: *A particularly unique vehicle in the post-war AFS inventory was the Transportable Water Unit (TWU) or Bikini Unit, the prototype of which was built on a Bedford S-Type chassis and assigned to the Civil Defence College at Reigate.* J. C. Thompson collection

Bottom Left: *Apart from the prototype, all the AFS TWUs were thereafter built on the Commer Superpoise chassis. This photograph shows one of the rafts assembled and equipped with its cargo of three portable pumps, one of which was used to propel the craft.* N.Tarling collection

They were to be self-propelled units carrying a rear-mounted pump delivering nine hundred gallons per minute and fitted with a reciprocating primer. The pump was to be mounted onto a Bedford five-ton chassis and was to carry a four hundred gallon water tank, two hose reels fed by the main pump and a lightweight portable pump as well as an extension ladder and the smaller items of equipment. The lightweight pump carried in a side locker was of a 'new and outstanding' design, weighing a little over three hundredweight with a capacity of exceeding 260-gallons per minute.

On 4th November 1953 it was announced that one hundred fire-fighting mobile columns, each with about 900 personnel and 50 pumps or associated vehicles would be the suggested quota for the defence of Great Britain in event of World War III. However, the quotas of vehicles and personnel changed frequently in the light of experience. This statement coincided with the unveiling of a new generation of fire appliances for atomic warfare at the Fire Service College at Dorking, Surrey during which a demonstration was given to newspaper representatives, fire officers and Her Majesty's Chief Inspector of Fire Services.

It was here that the illustrious Green Goddess first made an appearance together with other appliances of a mobile column, including a control unit equipped with a high powered multi-channel VHF radio set for communications with control rooms. They also had a low powered multi-channel set for contact between officers commanding the columns of five companies, each with ten self-propelled pumps and other ancillary vehicles.

Also introduced was a new hose-layer, capable of laying specially designed six-inch hose at the rate of 30mph and lightweight polythene and aluminium piping, six-inches in diameter that could be coupled direct to a six-inch outlet of a Green Goddess. Guests were also invited to view a kitchen van, and a foam tender, along with a new Maintenance Van with hinged sides enclosing workbenches. These prototype appliances, designed to replace the multitude of war-time standard appliances, were the fore runner of a large and ongoing range of appliances that would see service with the Auxiliary Fire Service until its disbandment, and in many cases far beyond that.

The Green Goddess emergency pump (EP) is now the most widely recognised and well known of the appliances that were used in the mobile column, predominantly because of their length of service and the multitude of uses these appliances have had since the AFS disbanded in 1968. The first EPs to be produced were based on the Bedford SHZ 4x2 chassis fitted with a standard Bedford six cylinder 110hp petrol engine and were equipped with a 900-gpm Sigmund FN4 single stage rear-mounted pump.

One aluminium 35' extension ladder was carried on the roof and a new addition to the fire-fighting inventory was the provision of a special locker accommodating a Coventry-Climax demountable pump of 350gpm capacity. A cradle was fitted that allowed lowering to ground level for easy removal and reloading whilst a two-wheeled carriage was provided for transporting the pump where the ground surface permitted. Hose comprised of 1,600' of two and three-quarter-inch rubber lined delivery hose stored in rolled up lengths and two hose reels each containing 180' of rubber tubing. Without doubt these new 'atomic' fire engines were as good, if not better than any regular appliance being produced by the manufacturers of the day. The length of time that they would subsequently be in service with other users has more than testified to the efficiency of the original design.

Top Right: *The Bikini Unit carried nine featherweight pumps and three inflatable rafts. An 'A' frame derrick assembly was used to load and unload the pumps as demonstrated by this Durham County Fire Brigade unit.* CD&DFRA

Bottom Right *One of the Bikini rafts showing the featherweight pump and short length of hose to which was affixed a nozzle and wooden tiller that were used to steer and propel the craft.* CD&DFRA

Above: *In addition to its uses for the Bikini Unit, the Commer Superpoise was also employed as a general-purpose lorry, personnel carrier and hose-layer. This personnel carrier was attached to Northumberland County Fire Brigade.* NFRS

Later EPs were built on the Bedford RLHZ 4x4 chassis, as these had a considerably greater ground clearance, which was necessary for gaining access to supposed debris ridden zones on the outskirts of bombed areas. There were other differences to the original design, notably the open hose reel locker was relocated to the centre of the body as opposed to above the rear wheel arches on the original version. Furthermore, the water tank capacity was reduced to three hundred gallons as opposed to four hundred gallons on the earlier version.

The production of these appliances was both a massive and welcome order to the chassis builders, body builders and fire engineering companies of the early post-war years. Indeed, it would prove to be so large that it could not be handled by one single manufacturer, nor even a small collection of them. Over five thousand chassis were eventually supplied with complete examples bodied by various companies including Harrington, Hoskins, Jennings, Papworth Industries, Park Royal, Plaxton, Strachan, Weymann, Whitson, Willowbrook and Windover. Beyond the Home Office contracts, the British Army ordered a further 135 examples and others were even exported to Southern Ireland.

All of the new issues were finished in a bronze green livery, selected to lessen the risk of identification by hostile aircraft.

For the proposed mobile column to be self-sufficient, a host of other unique appliances needed to be constructed. On the Bedford 4x2 and 4x4 chassis there was also a General Purpose Lorry (GPL), which as the name suggested had a multitude of variations. All basically featured drop-side wagon bodies with canvas tilt covers, adaptable for different uses they resembled similar units in use with the armed forces, apart from the orange flashing blinker lights affixed to the cab roof.

Some of these were used as personnel carriers in which the rear body was fitted out with an arrangement of three rows of wooden 'park bench' type seats to accommodate 28 people in addition to the driver and officer in charge who were carried in the cab. pipe-carriers based on the same chassis carried one-third of a mile of six-inch diameter plastic hose or light alloy piping, separated into 16' lengths, held in place by side supports and a large timber bulkhead to the front of the body.

With the aluminium piping and associated connecting pieces, it was possible to construct a pipe bridge over a roadway whereby water could be transported across roads without interfering with the movement of other appliances and for this purpose. The same principle could be applied to railways and navigable waterways, although in the case of the former a British Railways Bridge Inspector had to be used as the erecting supervisor. Bridging Parts Carrier vehicles were devised to carry enough piping and fittings to construct six bridges. Under-slung side lockers accommodated all of the aluminium couplings needed to connect the hoses to each other.

Below: *Dedicated AFS stations were not a common feature of the post-war AFS, as many regular brigades had sufficient accommodation in existing premises. This station was situated at Norton, Sheffield.* J. C. Thompson collection

Top Left: *Plymouth had particular good facilities as seen in this photograph where five 4x2 Green Goddesses are housed at the towns Embankment station.* J. C. Thompson collection

Middle Left: *Long wheelbase Austin Gypsy models were ordered in large numbers for use as personnel carriers and radio repeater units. This one was assigned to Croydon Fire Brigade and has since been acquired for preservation.* N. Tarling

Bottom Left: *The Austin Gipsy radio repeater units were equipped with twin radio transmitting and receiving sets, a generator and two sets of portable aerials.* J. C. Thompson

The hose-laying lorries contained half a mile of six-inch flexible hose, which would have been increased to one mile in an Emergency situation. This was made up with 35 folded lengths carried on each side of the body, separated by a longitudinal dividing wall. This could be paid out from the rear at speeds of up to 25mph. Rubber covers were fitted over the couplings to prevent damage as the hose was being paid out. Another variation was the 'Ramps, Dam and Hose Carrier', which, as the name suggested carried inflatable plastic-covered nylon portable dams of 2,500 or 5,000 gallons capacity and hose ramps which allowed vehicles to pass over engorged hoses without damaging or interrupting the water supply.

The hose-layer, pipe-carrier and ramps/dam and hose-carrier variations all had the function of relaying and supplying water over long distances, as it was envisaged that a future attack would either sever or disrupt mains water supplies. In order to test the water relay equipment, new drill procedures were devised and many exercises were undertaken to test its efficiency. *Exercise Kingston* in Hull in September 1953 was such an exercise during which a quarter of a mile of six-inch piping was put down and operated. In June of the following year a four and a half hour exercise at Bradford evaluated the equipment and two miles of six-inch plastic piping was laid in 90-minutes, after which there was complete satisfaction that the equipment could supply any amount of water needed for fire-fighting much quicker than had been expected.

In London 450 auxiliaries from Croydon, East Ham, Hertfordshire, Kent, London, Middlesex, Surrey and West Ham with 65 pumps and twelve pipe-lorries took part in a large scale water relay exercise, the objective of which was to gain experience in relaying large quantities of water and to study the effects of the operations on the flow of vehicular traffic.

The exercise saw eight lines of the new plastic piping providing for 32 fire-fighting jets, whilst (as a comparison) ten lines of the standard two and a half inch hose could only provided water for 20 jets. The Grand Union Canal was the convenient water supply on this occasion and the pipelines were laid in Bloomfield Road and Maida-Vale.

Petrol to supply the vehicles incorporated in a mobile column was a major consideration and some General Purpose Lorries (GPLs) undertook the function of petrol carriers on which steel racks were fitted on each side of the body to carry two tiers of petrol in jerry-can containers. Foam carriers were another variation of the GPL and carried one hundred, five-gallon cylindrical drums of foam concentrate on a three-tiered wooden framework of which the containers could be accessed from a central isle or from the outside of the vehicle by opening up the canvas covers. The necessary foam branches were accommodated in external lockers.

Also based on Bedford chassis, both 4x2 and 4x4 versions, were vehicles with communications facilities. The control unit featured the standard Bedford cab with a large box body on the back. Internally this was fitted out with VHF radio equipment, a ten-line telephone switchboard, large-scale wall maps and mobilising boards, plus desks and chairs for the operators. They were recognised by a red and white chequered band around the top of the body and an illuminating plastic red and white chequered dome on the cab roof, universally signifying the vehicle's use as a fire ground control point. A similar unit was the Communications Unit, which had a similar box type body but lacked the red and white identification markings and featured fewer windows in the saloon compartment.

Top Right: *Land Rover models were also ordered in huge numbers for use by the AFS and Civil Defence and were characterised by the twin orange flashing lights on the bonnet. This one was pictured at Moreton-in-Marsh in 1967.*

Middle Right: *As well as being used for general personnel carriers, the Land Rover also had a useful function as field telephone units with a trailer carrying drums of cable and poles for carrying the cable over obstructions.*

Bottom Right: *Not as prevalent as the short wheelbase models, were the long wheelbase Land Rover Safari personnel carriers. These models were being delivered right up until the last days of the existence of the AFS. This one was issued in 1962. J. C. Thompson collection*

Top Left: *The smallest vehicles in a mobile column were the motorbikes used by the despatch riders. Predominantly of Matchless make, one of the riders watches the proceedings as a Commer hose-layer pays out its load of six-inch hose.* N. Tarling collection

Middle Left: *The movement of mobile columns during exercises must have caused much disruption to other road users with vehicles commonly being stretched out over distances of up to three miles.*

Bottom Left: *In Suffolk the crew of a pipe-carrier get to work laying a temporary water main. The fireman on the right with the war-time helmet is holding one of the 'victaulic' couplings used to join each length of pipe.* N.Tarling collection

These vehicles were used to carry spare parts and facilities for the maintenance of radio and field telephone equipment and carried generators for charging radio batteries on vehicles so equipped. There were other essential support vehicles constructed for convoy duties such as maintenance vans, catering vehicles, stores vans and mobile kitchens. The latter vehicle was characterised by a large upwards-hinged side panel giving access to the food and providing a convenient shelter. These highly essential vehicles also towed a box trailer to carry the coal that was needed to fire the cooking ranges.

As well as the Bedford make, Commer models also formed a major part of the heavy vehicles in the AFS fleet. Three hundred of these large ungainly forward-control Q4 Superpoise 4x4 vehicles were ordered in April 1954. In a similar manner to the Bedfords, there were hose-layers, hose-carriers, personnel carriers and most unusual and unique for the time, a vehicle designed for carrying small boats, the Transportable Water Unit (TWU) or Bikini Unit. This vehicle carried three inflatable rubber rafts manufactured by R.F.D. Ltd., of Godalming and were of the type developed for air-sea rescue operations.

The rafts were contained in three large canvas cylindrical bags stored on a metal gantry over the cab roof. These rafts were developed for the Home Office by the Chief Fire Officer of Kent Fire Brigade after examining a wheelwright raft as used by the Royal Navy. The evaluation TWU appliance, based on a Bedford 4x2 chassis, was first demonstrated on the River Mole near Dorking in October 1954. Weighing 320lbs and capable of being inflated by carbon dioxide in 30-seconds, each raft could carry three featherweight pumps, one of which was also used as the motive power and steering gear of the boat.

By connecting a short length of tubing and branch pipe to one of the deliveries, a jet of water was projected over the stern, thus propelling the craft at speeds of up to six knots. The raft was so designed that in the event of the lower floats being punctured the upper floats were still sufficient to keep the craft afloat. Just in case, a puncture repair outfit was carried on each raft. There was also a separate foot and hand operated bellows, in the event that the former system did not work. The complete unit carried nine featherweight pumps, three for each boat and included an 'A' frame derrick assembly on the rear of the vehicle to aid with the loading and unloading of the equipment.

It was therefore possible to position the vehicle on a bridge and lower the boats into the water over the parapet, as the derrick assembly operated over the rear or swivelled through 90° to off-load from the side. The Bikini name was not derived from the swimsuit or the island in the Pacific, but from the name of the Managing Director of the manufacturer Mr. A. Van Beugen Bik; having been suggested by Lt. Commander J. H. Fordham, Chief Fire Officer of Kent. The concept behind the design was for a vehicle capable of pumping large volumes of water, usually from inaccessible sources of open water. These, problems had been evident during the London Blitz, when trailer pumps or self-propelled pumps could not gain access to the Thames at low tide because of the mud banks. Consequently, the Bikini Unit would save equipment such as fixed pumps on bridges, as had occurred in war-time London, because the rafts could be used irrespective of the state of the tide.

Top Right: *An unusual and little known mode of transport for AFS officers was this Morris mini van pictured at Wallsend, Northumberland in 1966, just after delivery. It was assigned to the paid officer who was responsible for the brigade's AFS contingent.* Ian Moore

Middle Right *Equally unusual in the AFS fleet was this Thornycroft Nubian recovery vehicle that was based at the Fire Service Training Centre, Moreton-in-Marsh. The crane on this one was later remounted onto a more modern civilian appliance.* J. C. Thompson collection

Bottom Right: *Some Bedford emergency recovery units of standard army pattern were also assigned to the AFS. After the organisation disbanded almost the entire batch was bought by regular fire brigades to reappear in the livery of the host brigade, although Cornwall retained the olive green livery of their example.* J. C .Thompson collection

Above: *A trio of land Rovers, one of them the transport of the column commander, are seen together with a despatch rider's motor cycle at an exercise in the sea front car park just off the promenade at South Shields (then in County Durham) back in 1965.* D. Barker collection

Ironically, three months after the public demonstration, Kent Fire Brigade had cause to use one of the Bikini Units in anger when Her Majesty's Submarine *Talent* ran aground on the River Medway, resulting in the loss of life of four dockyard workers from the Naval Dockyard at Chatham. During the salvage and 'pumping-out operation' the prototype Bikini unit, by then based at Reigate was mobilised to the incident to aid with the transportation of pumps that were needed on the mud bank where salvage operations were ongoing; thus demonstrating the effectiveness of the concept.

Many hundreds of Land Rovers were ordered by the Home Office for use with the Civil Defence and AFS, most being of the short wheel base variety with canvas tops. These were just like those used by the armed forces, with the exception of a twin orange flashing light unit mounted on the front of the bonnet. These vehicles had various purposes, such as for use as staff cars or for reconnaissance work and communications duties.

Those assigned to communications duties were usually attached to a two-wheeled 'Brockhouse' trailer, which contained field telephone equipment and cable drums for laying out field telephone lines. The ladder on the side was to aid with the placement of the telephone cables and not for fire-fighting purposes. Less common were Land Rover Safari personnel carriers, some of which were still being delivered in the 1960s. Austin Gipsy's were also used in large numbers, but these were usually of the hard top variety.

As well as having the same functions as the Land Rovers, one particular use for the Gipsy was a radio repeater unit. These vehicles carried two radio transmitting/receiving sets, generators and aerials. One more type of vehicle worthy of mention is the breakdown/recovery vehicle. Two types were issued; the first five were based, unusually on Thornycroft Nubian chassis fitted with a Harvey Frost crane of five-ton capacity. Thereafter ten of the more 'rugged' Bedford RL 4x4 chassis were obtained, and these were of the same pattern of wheeled light recovery vehicle as used by the Army. The crane on these vehicles had three-tons lifting capacity and a seven-ton main winch. They were the least common of the post-war standard Civil Defence vehicles.

Having briefly described the principle types of vehicles used by the post-war AFS, there were many other less numerous types such as the early Austin A40 Devon estate cars and later Bedford CA Dormobile passenger-carrying vehicles. Then came the plethora of motor cycles for use by despatch riders, whose responsibility was reconnaissance and ensuring the smooth passage of convoys; post-war the motorcycles were mostly of Matchless or AJS make.

The impressive new 'atomic fire engines' were allocated to local authority fire brigades in England, Wales and Northern Ireland according to the risks and the amount of volunteers. Naturally the bigger establishments had a greater amount and variety of appliances. In association with the new generation of appliances, there were still pre-war vehicles on the establishment and in some cases trailer pump towing vehicles and war-time canteen vans remained on strength until the 1960s.

Top Right: *Nottingham City had a purpose built garage to house its AFS appliances. This 1955 line up includes a control unit, a Bikini unit, a Land Rover and a brace of emergency pumps. J. C. Thompson collection*

Middle Right: *AFS personnel were adept at improvisation and weekend camps were a regular feature of the training program. In County Durham, during an exercise at Hamsterley Forest, the crew of a former war-time Austin canteen van are clearing up having satisfied the appetites of the hungry volunteers. G. & A. Pringle*

Bottom Right: *Also in Hamsterley Forest, a 4x4 Green Goddess has shown its off-road capabilities by negotiating the steep inclines of a disused quarry to act as base pump in a water relay exercise. G. & A. Pringle*

Accommodation of the vehicles and personnel was often a pressing concern. In some areas AFS appliances, especially the emergency pumps were housed in appliance rooms alongside a local authority brigade's regular machines, in other cases additional garages were constructed at the rear of fire stations. Yet, as was often the case, the appliances often stood out in the open at fire station yards. Some brigades had separate fire stations built for the AFS contingent such as at Bedlington, Northumberland and Bebington in Cheshire. Durham County Fire Brigade's AFS appliances were housed in pre-fabricated garages, which were dismantled and re-erected at other sites on different occaions.

Below: *Moreton-in-Marsh, was the main centre of training for AFS personnel. Fleets of appliances were stored in former aircraft hangars, one of which can be seen in this photograph taken in 1967, the last full year of the existence of the AFS.*

Liverpool Fire Brigade was particularly keen to give the city's auxiliary's greater experience and set up an AFS station at Princes Dock, manned five nights each week from where the crews were permitted to attend nearby fires. In August 1954 the AFS moved into a new headquarters and training centre at the Towers, Belvidere Road. Opened by Her Majesty's Inspector of Fire Services, the three-storey detached house featured ample facilities, not provided at the previous overcrowded base at the city's Hatton Garden station.

In Northumberland the fire authority set up a camp on Forestry Commission land in Kielder Forest, where frequent weekend training courses took place with both the regular and auxiliary staff from several of the north eastern fire brigades. This facility not only offered an ideal training environment as far as terrain and water supplies went, but it also offered useful insurance in case of the outbreak of fire in Europe's biggest man-made forestry plantation.

Uniforms supplied to the AFS varied from authority to authority, but certainly included basic fire kit comprising of tunic, trousers, helmet and axe, wet legs, wellington boots, helmet and overalls. On the arms of the tunic was a red embroidered AFS badge. Initially the helmet consisted of the war-time 'soup dish' steel-type, but progressively either NATO-type steel helmets or conventional fire helmets were issued, supposedly! In one northeastern fire brigade the AFS personnel were still being issued with NATO-style helmets and obsolete National Fire Service cap badges, some 20-years after that organisation ceased to be.

Large-scale exercises continued to form a great part of the training commitments of the AFS and in October 1957 five hundred men and women AFS volunteers from nine counties took part in a large-scale exercise at Hyde Park in the centre of London.

Above: *Three 4x4 Bedford R-Type personnel carriers await their crews at Moreton-in-Marsh in 1967, just a year before disbandment. Personnel in the rear body were seated on longitudinal wooden park bench type seats.*

Ninety-two AFS appliances from the region were mobilised in two columns before converging on Hyde Park. Then followed a spectacular exercise at Dell Bridge where 60 pumps on either side of the Serpentine and three on the bridge itself provided a curtain of water from 150 jets.

Congratulating those taking part afterward, General Sir Sydney Kirkman, Director-General of Civil Defence reminded all that fire remained one of the greatest hazards of war and that much had been done to explain to the public what could be done provided the country had the 'right equipment, techniques and the manpower.'

These big exercises, held in the hearts of cities and towns did much to publicise the invariably unseen work of the many dedicated volunteers. They would also stimulate more members of the public to enroll and were thus a common feature of the duty periods for the volunteers. In late 1965, a joint AFS and Army exercise took place at the Central Ammunition Depot, Longtown, Cumberland, involving a one hundred vehicle mobile column assembled from various parts of the East and West Ridings of Yorkshire. At Longtown the AFS were joined by officers and men of various Territorial Army Regiments and the Army Fire Service after which an exercise involving water relaying using Bikini rafts, pipe bridges and portable dams was carried out to prove the value of the training that the members of the TA had undergone in emergency fire-fighting.

Without doubt the biggest exercise ever held by the Civil Defence was *Exercise Tercentenary* which took place in September 1966 and saw five thousand AFS personnel from 118 fire brigades converge on the Royal Victoria and Royal Albert docks in the East End of London. The impressive force was deployed in ten columns to tackle simulated fires during which 600 water jets were operated at one time . Equipment brought into play included ten miles of six-inch hose and twelve miles of six-inch pipe, 25 inflatable dams, 96 heavy and 108 light pumps and 42 Bikini rafts. An interesting prelude to the exercise was an expedition taken by two Bikini rafts, each with a light pump and a three man crew that made the long journey from Braunston near Rugby, Warwickshire to London via the Grand Union Canal, a distance of 130 miles that involved travelling through 101 locks. A van with bedding accompanied the rafts, allowing the crews to camp in tents at night.

The crafts entered the River Thames at Brentford and sailed up to London Fire Brigade's fireboat station at Woolwich, from where they then took part in the exercise. Appliances at this exercise travelled from as far away as Northumberland and Cumberland. The personnel were accommodated at five base camps, established at the RAF bases at Cardington and Hendon and the army barracks at Woolwich, Gravesend and Vange.

In late-1967 more than 230 regular, retained or AFS men and women from Birmingham, Coventry, Herefordshire , Solihull, Warwickshire and Worcester City and County took part in a weekend exercise at Nesscliffe Army Camp near Shrewsbury. A column of 53 vehicles was assembled with the objective of proceeding the three miles from base to the fireground, where they provided a total of 20 jets of water covering a fire front of one mile. Water was taken from the river, half a mile distant and involved setting up water relays, man-handling ten light portable base pumps with associated equipment down a 30' vertical drop and across a meadow to the river where a bridge was erected and two inflatable dams set up.

Above: *The refuelling of mobile column vehicles was accommodated in times of war by adopted general purpose lorries/petrol carriers supplemented when necessary by vehicles from the petroleum refining companies.*

The AFS and Civil Defence were on a sound foundation and there was plenty of evidence that the idea behind the mobilisation and assembly of both organisations in times of crisis, with the ability to work professionally in conjunction with the other emergency services had paid off.

Much benefit had been achieved in both organisations through continuous training and frequent exercises. In fact, in 1966 it was remarked by Her Majesty's Inspector of Fire Services that, following a review of home defence the Government would continue to support the Fire Service in its emergency preparations including the maintenance of the AFS. In reality, Harold Wilson's Government had other plans as more serious discussions were taking place behind closed doors and the Civil Defence services were to be the first casualties.

DISBANDMENT

Early in 1968 the House of Commons approved by 291 votes to 233, the Government's proposals to disband the AFS and the Civil Defence Corps. During the debate, the Home Secretary advised that future stockpiling of emergency fire equipment would cease but the Fire Service would continue emergency planning and there would still be some training undertaken at Moreton-in-Marsh. Stocks of equipment would be retained and the country's 350 full time officers assigned with the responsibility of looking after the AFS would be absorbed into regular brigades. All recruitment and the construction of new accommodation was suspended, and all training was to cease by the end of March. The United Kingdom civil defence organisation was to be stood down forthwith.

On hearing this shock announcement, many AFS volunteers expressed a willingness to continue to provide a volunteer service for no annual bounty. Whilst the Government was grateful for the offer, the payment (£10 per annum) only amounted to 8.5% of the cost of the AFS. The annual costs at the time being almost one and a half million pounds of which the bounty and expenses accounted for just £110,000; the bounty alone would not produce the savings required.

Above: *Demonstrating their supporting role to fire services, a batch of no less than seven Green Goddesses (a mix of 4x4 and 4x2 units) are set to pump thousands of gallons of water onto an underground coal mine fire in 1966.* NFRS

There was naturally much indignation at this surprise announcement and very soon after nearly 2,000 Civil Defence workers and 150 AFS members representing more than 50 local authorities held a march in London to protest against the decision. Also in support of the volunteers, the County Council Association protested to the Home Secretary about its concern over his 'care and maintenance' plan for civil defence.

A Motion was tabled in the Commons by a group of Conservative MPs calling for the Government to reconsider its decision to disband the AFS and Civil Defence Corps, as it would deprive thousands of volunteers of their right to train and serve in a role that had been recognised as a necessary part of the policy of deterrent against the threat of nuclear war, and which had already saved the lives of many of their fellow countrymen in peace-time. Despite a joint deputation from the CCA, the Association of Municipal Corporations and the Greater London Council, the Home Secretary was not prepared to re-consider the Government's decision.

At the time the nation's annual fire losses amounted to eighty million pounds, but according to the Government the relationship of the AFS to those losses just did not exist because the AFS did no peace-time fire duties. Amongst the many letters of protest against the decision, one particular letter in support of the 'stand-down' generated many criticisms. A letter in the fire press and subsequent reproduction in the national press from a north eastern Chief Fire Officer opined, that the Fire Brigade was "well rid of our amateur brothers" and the decisions to disband the AFS was the best thing that had happened to the British fire services in the last 20-years. The critic described the AFS personnel as hobbyists graduated to tradesmen who considered themselves as good as, if not better than, their masters. It further stated that the organisation was suffered by many chief officers but never accepted and needed total re-organisation and replacement by a new organisation with a new name such as Fire Service Reserve.

Naturally this opinion resulted in the receipt of many letters of reply from serving fire officers supporting the retention of the Civil Defence Fire Service. One Chief Fire Officer declared that the AFS had 'had a raw deal at the hands of the Government' and publicly expressed appreciation and admiration for the work that had been done, which was surely echoed by the majority of colleagues in the service. The critical letter writer did not stand alone however, and another Chief Fire Officer was quite convinced that the country 'would be able to cope with any future emergency of the scale of the *Torrey Canyon* disaster, considering that the AFS were only in attendance during the first 48-hours.' Even so he wrote that the loss of AFS equipment 'was another matter altogether, and might prove to be a problem as the Green Goddesses were very valuable!'

Top Right: *Tynemouth Fire Brigade was allocated a pair of 4x2 Goddesses for the duration of the AFS existence. Upon disbandment this example was repainted yellow and gave further service as a road accident vehicle.*

Middle Right: *This AFS general-purpose vehicle dates from 1967, the chrome trim on the grille denoting a later model. Just one year later the AFS ceased to exist.*
J. C. Thompson collection

Bottom Right: *Another late-model general-purpose lorry. This 1965 model was adapted as a petrol carrier and was recognisable by the bumper-mounted cylinders that contained two foam fire extinguishers.* J. C. Thompson collection

Top Left: *Later style personnel-carrying vehicles were based on Bedford CA chassis. This MkII CA at Moreton-in-Marsh dates from 1966.* J. C. Thompson collection

Middle Left: *Despite the ongoing delivery of new appliances for the AFS, war-time ATVs soldiered on until the end in 1968. This pair, still in the original primer undercoat, were still in service when photographed at Moreton-in-Marsh in 1967.*

Bottom Left: *Large numbers of Green Goddesses were mobilised in an oil spill clearing up operation following the grounding of the MV* Torrey Canyon *off Cornwall in 1967.* J. C. Thompson collection

Regardless of the discussions, arguments and counter-arguments, the AFS and the Civil Defence was doomed. At midnight on 31st March 1968, the organisation was no more. Whilst mention was made that the AFS did no peace-time duties of course they did. Many brigades allowed the personnel to attend fires either in the regular appliances or accompanying the regular crews with Green Goddesses. This role was frowned upon as far back as 1952, when the issue was raised at the Cleethorpes Fire Brigades Union Conference, where proposals were made that all possible steps should be taken to prevent AFS personnel from forming crews at normal peace-time fires. 'They should not be used as a measure of affecting economies against the interests of the professional fire service.'

On selected nights each week and at weekends, the AFS members reported for duty and attended fires as and when required, usually in a supernumerary capacity. There were many incidents that the AFS attended. Many services called the personnel in to assist with major fires or special service calls releasing some of the regular appliances to return and provide additional fire cover. There were numerous occasions when the Green Goddesses gave legendary service.

One incident when the AFS came to the fore occurred in Northumberland in 1966, when Lynemouth Colliery suffered a major underground fire that threatened the future of coal production. Despite the efforts of 22 pumps from the coal board and the attendance of the NCB's Rescue Brigade, the fire burned on and eventually the local authority was called. Within a short time seven Green Goddesses were mobilised and with these additional resources 750,000-gallons of water were pumped down the mine. The AFS appliances worked non-stop and were manned by volunteers, many of whom had to attend their normal places of employment the next day.

Above: *Appliances from Lancashire made the long journey to the Royal Docks, London for* Exercise Tercentary. *It would appear that a considerable time would have to be expended when the time came to make up all of the hose lines.*

The London AFS also attended fires as required, supporting their regular colleagues as dedicated volunteers. A typical example being a major factory fire that occurred at Greenford Industrial Estate in early 1967, at which 14 emergency pumps with AFS crews supplemented the 18 regular London Fire Brigade appliances. A total of 30 jets were used to extinguish the fire. Coincidentally, four days later the Fire Brigade were back at the same estate for another major fire at which three AFS crews supplemented fifteen other pumps and crews in order to extinguish this second fire.

The *Torrey Canyon* oil tanker disaster in the English Channel in March 1967 was a prolonged operation requiring the delivery of thousands of gallons of water to wash away crude oil deposits on the beaches of Cornwall, when the grounded vessel and its 117,000 ton cargo of crude oil started leaking from the damaged hull. On occasions AFS vehicles including 26 Green Goddesses from Devon, Exeter, Plymouth and Somerset were mobilised to the County.

At one time the total reinforcing strength mobilised to the incident stood at 300 personnel and 46 Green Goddesses with ancillary vehicles in the form of personnel carriers, command cars, mobile workshops and canteen vans. This particular incident occurring in the last full year of the exitence of a nation-wide Civil Defence force demonstrated the epitomy of the advantages of such a useful resource being readily available at such short notice; not only for fires but for other disatsers. However, as far as the Government was concerned, the AFS was only there for use in times of war, and as the threat had now diminished, spending cuts had to be made and that was that. After 20-years of diligent service the Civil Defence and AFS organisations were no more.

Top Left: Exercise Tercentary, *held in commemoration of the great fire of London, was the largest exercise ever held by the post-war AFS. This picture depicts vehicles from Newcastle-upon-Tyne and Carlisle that made the long journey to the capital to participate in the event.*

Middle Left: *An overall photographic view of one of the assembly points at* Exercise Tercentary. *The Green Goddess in the centre is getting an unplanned wash from a ruptured length of hose.*

Bottom Left: *Three AFS appliances, including a war-time Austin ATV, are pictured laid up in the yard of a Newcastle-upon-Tyne fire station in 1968, as they await collection by Home Office agents for eventual disposal or storage*

At the time of disbandment there were approximately 10,436 men and 2,665 women attached to the AFS in England and Wales and 663 men and 133 women in Scotland. At the stroke of midnight on 31st March 1968, all were stood down and the AFS appliances laid up in fire station yards throughout the country pending disposal (often by auction or sealed tender) or removal for storage at Government depots. Where a local authority had a special reason for retaining some of the appliances and equipment, the Home Secretary was disposed to grant them an opportunity to hire or purchase such items.

Naturally, the Green Goddess was a popular and economical buy and many were quickly acquired by regular brigades for use as water tenders or for placing in the reserve fleet. So it was that Goddesses thereafter appeared in any colour but green. There were white ones in the West Riding of Yorkshire, yellow ones in Coventry and York, red ones all over the place and even a maroon one in Leicestershire. Glamorgan in Wales bought some and converted them to foam tenders finishing them in an attractive white over red livery.

Many other vehicles were sold to dealers like L.W. Vass in Ampthill, Bedfordshire or Jacksons at Misson near Doncaster who refurbished them and exported some overseas; others were scrapped for spare parts or sold on to industrial fire brigades. Thereafter the ubiquitous Green Goddess saw service with fire brigades throughout the world including Cyprus, Australia, New Zealand, Iceland and the Caribbean. Of the other major types of AFS appliances not many saw second careers with Fire Brigades. Some of the Bedford control units were acquired by regular fire brigades such as Dorset, Hereford & Worcester and Tayside, as were some Civil Defence Ford Thames signals units.

The odd Bedford or Commer hose-layers saw second careers also, but the remaining huge fleet of appliances were returned to the various stores throughout the country until being periodically sold off at Government auctions. Surprisingly, few Bikini units saw second careers. The South Eastern Fire Brigade took up the offer and acquired one, complete with the nine pumps for the sum of £1,690.

The 1968 Home Office rate for Green Goddesses, complete with equipment was £790. Ten years later, Vass in Bedfordshire were charging up to £3,400 for a refurbished 4x4 goddess. When considering the large numbers of war-time and peace-time civil defence vehicles, notably the ATVs and other NFS standard appliances, very few survived into preservation; especially the ATVs of which many were still part of the Home Office stock as late as 1968.

This, then is the end of the saga of the illustrious Auxiliary Fire Service. Yet the lifespan of the vehicles, not dissimilar to the cult of the stored steam locomotives at Dai Woodham's scrapyard in Wales, will ensure that the name of the organisation, perpetuated by the vehicles that remain will ensure that for the rest of eternity the organisation will never pass entirely into the history books. This history is therefore graciously dedicated to all those men and women that gave up their time and in some cases their lives for the noblest of causes.

Below: *The British Army Fire Service was the only other organisation to order 4x4 emergency pumps of the standard Civil Defence pattern. Their appliances were characterised by the more up-dated front grille assembly and a slightly different locker configuration at the rear.* N. Tarling collection

ACKNOWLEDGEMENTS

Particular thanks are due to John C. Thompson, joint author of the fascinating book *The Green Machines,* for his hospitality and free use of photographs in his collection. For without these illustrations and his technical support, this book would not have been as comprehensive. Also Norman Tarling for his unceasing support and free access to his photograph archive.

Thanks are also owed to Dennis Barker, Brett Clayton, Jeff Clish, Ian Moore, Ian Scott, Trevor Welham, County Durham and Darlington Fire & Rescue Authority (CDDFRA) and Northumberland Fire & Rescue Service (NFRS) for their hospitality over the years and for access to their photographic archives and all others who have assisted and shared in a mutual appreciation of the Auxiliary Fire Service.

Above: *Despite still carrying standard Home Office AFS livery, this Huddersfield Green Goddess was pictured at a grass fire near Marsden in 1969, long after the AFS was formally disbanded. Although a more than fitting 'end picture' in its own right, this picture will undoubtedly please the editor, who also hails from this part of the West Riding.*

OTHER FIRE SERVICE BOOKS IN THE NOSTALGIA ROAD SERIES

British Fire Engines of the 1950s & '60s	Simon Rowley
Fire Engines of North West England	Robert F. Bonner
Fire Engines of North East England	Ron Henderson
and coming soon	
Airport Crash Tenders	Ron Henderson